Praise for **Ready for the Day!** and the ParentSmart/KidHappy™ Series:

"Stacey Kaye has created a must-have series that will make life easier for parents and their children. In a delightfully entertaining way, kids will learn from a very early age skills to resolve typical, everyday struggles—skills they will take with them for the rest of their lives."

—**Myrna B. Shure, Ph.D.**, author of *Raising a Thinking Child* and *Thinking Parent, Thinking Child*

"The story focuses on encouraging cooperation in young children and clearly reminds parents that even through a frenzied morning routine, it's important to 'stop, look, and listen' to children. That's when family life really happens, after all."

—**Donna Erickson,** host of award-winning *Donna's Day* on public television, author of *Donna Erickson's Fabulous Funstuff for Families,* and syndicated newspaper columnist

"These books present important concepts to parents and children. They can help children learn to be aware of feelings and to engage in problem solving, key components of emotional intelligence. The explanation of these concepts at the end of the book is also important for parents to be able to generalize these skills to other areas of the child's life."

—**Steven Tobias, Psy.D.**, coauthor of *Emotionally Intelligent Parenting*

"ParentSmart/KidHappy is for any family looking for ways to get through those all-too-common everyday struggles. Reading these realistic stories together, kids and parents learn positive, hassle-free solutions to those universal battles."

—**Nancy Samalin, M.S.,** lecturer and best-selling author of *Loving Without Spoiling: And 100 Other Timeless Tips for Raising Terrific Kids*

"ParentSmart/KidHappy is a lifesaver for any stressed parent (do you know one who isn't?) who wants to ease daily battles and raise an emotionally healthy child."

—**Dr. Michele Borba,** author of *No More Misbehavin'* and *Parents Do Make a Difference*

Ready for the Day!

A Tale of Teamwork and Toast, and Hardly Any Foot-Dragging

by Stacey R. Kaye

illustrated by Elizabeth O. Dulemba

edited by Eric Braun

free spirit
PUBLiSHiNG®

Meeting kids'
social & emotional
needs since 1983

Library of Congress Cataloging-in-Publication Data
Kaye, Stacey R.
  Ready for the day! : a tale of teamwork and toast, and hardly any foot-dragging / by Stacey R. Kaye ; illustrated by Elizabeth O. Dulemba ; edited by Eric Braun.
      p. cm.
  ISBN-13: 978-1-57542-268-8
  ISBN-10: 1-57542-268-9
  1. Child rearing—Juvenile literature. 2. Morning—Juvenile literature. I. Dulemba, Elizabeth O., ill.
II. Braun, Eric, 1971– III. Title.
  HQ769.K344 2007
  649'.6—dc22

                                                                2007047961

Cover and interior design by Michelle Lee

10 9 8 7 6 5 4 3 2 1
Printed in China

Free Spirit Publishing Inc.
217 Fifth Avenue North, Suite 200
Minneapolis, MN 55401-1299
(612) 338-2068
help4kids@freespirit.com
www.freespirit.com

To Steven, Audrey, and Margo

Acknowledgments

Thank you to Judy Galbraith and Free Spirit Publishing for providing the opportunity to publish this series and for their tireless dedication to providing children, parents, and educators with books that make a difference.

Thank you to my editor, Eric Braun, for shaping my ideas into a story and bringing the language of positive parenting to life. Thank you to Elizabeth Dulemba for her beautiful illustrations.

Thank you to Michelle Fallon, LICSW, for reading drafts of the manuscript and providing valuable feedback.

Grown-ups: Some dialogue in this book is color-coded.
Green words validate feelings.
Blue words offer choices.
Red words encourage.
Learn more about these parenting techniques at the end of the book.

It's morningtime, and Maya is still sleepy.

"Good morning!" Daddy says. "Are you ready to start the day?"

"Noooooo," Maya whines. "I don't want to go to school today. I want to stay home with you."

Daddy kneels down next to Maya. "I know just how you feel," he says. "I wish we could spend the day together, too. Hey, I have an idea. Let's pick a game to play later when we get home."

Maya perks up. It feels good to know Daddy understands.

"Daddy, I know the best game."

"Let's play Bunny Party!" Maya shouts.

"Great! I'm excited to play this later," Daddy says.
"Now, let's get dressed so we
can eat breakfast."

"Would you like to wear your star shirt and shorts or your daisy-daisy dress?"

"I want to wear my daisy-daisy dress!" Maya says.

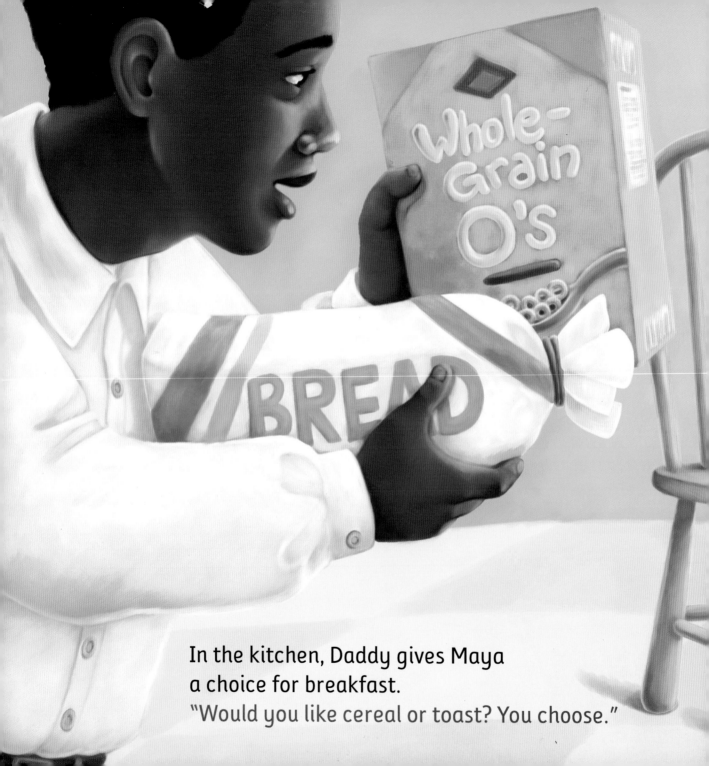

In the kitchen, Daddy gives Maya
a choice for breakfast.
"Would you like cereal or toast? You choose."

Maya shakes her head.
"I do *not* want cereal, and I do *not* want toast."

"It sounds like you're having trouble choosing," Daddy says.
"I'll pick this time, and you can choose next time. Let's have toast."

Maya thinks about that. "Can we have *peanut butter—banana* toast, please?"

"Yum! That sounds delicious," Daddy says. "And you remembered to say 'please'!"

After Daddy spreads the peanut butter, Maya puts bananas on top.

Daddy says, "Maya, your peanut butter–banana toast idea made this a delicious and healthy breakfast. Now we'll have energy for the day."

After breakfast, Maya helps clean up.
"We're a real team this morning," Daddy says.

Maya and Daddy have more to do to get ready for the day, so they hop like bunnies to the bathroom.

"Would you like to do your hair or brush your teeth first?" Daddy asks.

"Hair!" Maya says, and hands Daddy the barrettes.

"Wow, you're really cooperating today," Daddy says.

Maya has a hard time with the toothpaste, and some spills in the sink.

"Oh, man!" she says. "I'm not brushing my teeth today!"

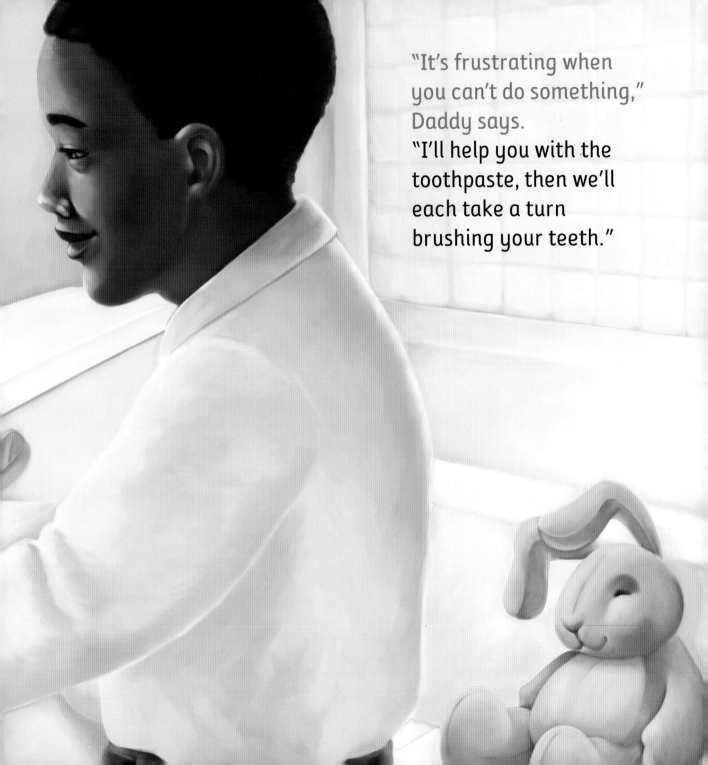

"It's frustrating when you can't do something," Daddy says.
"I'll help you with the toothpaste, then we'll each take a turn brushing your teeth."

"Your teeth are sparkling clean," Daddy says. "Now let's race to find your shoes."

"Here they are!" Maya calls when she finds them.

"All right! You found your sandals," Daddy says.

"We got ready so quickly, we still have ten minutes before we have to leave. Would you like to color a picture or play with Bunny? You choose."

"Yeah!" Maya cheers. "I'll do the bunny hop with Bunny! Come on, Daddy, follow me!"

Encouraging Cooperation
And Raising Confident, Emotionally Intelligent Children

As most parents and caregivers of preschool-age children know, transitions such as getting ready for the day can be very frustrating—especially when we're late or stressed out! Many of us have resorted to threatening timeouts, taking away a favorite toy or book, or bribing with rewards. While these techniques may seem natural, and may even get short-term results, they're probably not going to prevent the same struggle from arising again tomorrow morning. And none of these approaches teaches our kids to think for themselves or acknowledges that their feelings are important.

Of course, kids' feelings *are* important, even when they feel frustrated or mad—or when they just don't feel like going to school! Research shows that kids who believe the adults in their lives respect them and think they are important are more likely to cooperate during transitions. Those kids are *also* more likely to grow in self-esteem, independence, and emotional intelligence.

The term "emotional intelligence" refers to our ability to recognize emotions in ourselves and others and to manage our emotions. Experts such as Daniel Goleman, who has written several books on the subject, consider emotional intelligence a key to developing strong relationships, an optimistic outlook, self-confidence, and general happiness.

The important thing is to work *with* kids rather than manipulating them (with rewards or other methods). In this way, we can help them develop their emotional intelligence while we encourage them to cooperate during transitions. No book can tell you exactly what to say to the children in your life, but the following are basic guidelines recommended by psychologists and parenting experts.

Validate Feelings

Children who know that feelings are normal and feelings have names have an easier time managing and expressing them appropriately. Children who learn to recognize and manage their feelings also learn to have empathy for other people's feelings. In turn, these skills help kids improve social skills and do better in school.

It's important to acknowledge children's feelings even if you can't accommodate them. Letting kids know you understand how they feel shows that you think they and their feelings are important. A child who feels important is more likely to cooperate, have high self-esteem, and develop positive emotional health.

To help kids learn about emotions, talk with them about their feelings, your feelings, and the feelings of others. Recognize feelings, name them, and make it clear that all feelings are acceptable. It's fine, for example, to be disappointed that it's time for school or childcare. It's natural. However, not all ways of *showing* feelings are acceptable. You might say, "It's okay to feel disappointed. Hitting is not okay."

Parents and caregivers can set an example. If you feel tired, frustrated, proud, silly—talk about it. Show your child that no matter how you feel you can still be fair, considerate, and loving. When reading books, ask your child how a character in the story might be feeling. Encourage your child to think about the feelings of others.

Understanding a child's point of view is more important than fixing the problem. Be present, help label the feelings, be patient, and demonstrate acceptance (reserve judgment).

- You really miss Mommy, don't you? I'm sorry she's not home now. I miss her, too.
- I would feel the same way.
- Ouch! That must really hurt.
- It sounds like you are really angry.
- It can be disappointing when your friend won't share.

In the main part of this book, look for dialogue in green for other examples of validating feelings.

Offer Choices

Kids often feel powerless when grown-ups tell them what to do and what not to do. As a result, they may seek power by resisting you. Instead of commanding kids to do something, try offering a choice and watch them embrace the opportunity to feel in control of the situation. Giving kids choices empowers children and has several benefits. It takes the air out of power struggles so you can get things done without a battle. And the long-term benefits are even better. Children who are regularly given choices are more independent, more skilled at making decisions, and more aware of the relationship between their decisions and possible outcomes. Finally, and maybe most important, having choices makes kids feel good.

Giving up some power doesn't mean you stop being the adult. It means you look for parts of a situation that you are willing to let the child control. Be sure to offer appropriate choices. Kids aren't mature enough to choose their own bedtime, for example. Offer specific options: "Would you like to have cereal or toast?" Limit options to two or three for preschoolers.

Sometimes a child may seem overwhelmed by choices, or resist them altogether. When that happens, it's important for the adult to step in: "It looks like it's hard to choose right now. I'll decide this time and you can choose next time."

More examples:

- Would you like to take a bath or a shower?
- Which would you like to clean up first, the checkers game or this princess puzzle?
- Would you like me to help you tie your shoes or do you want to tie them yourself?
- Would you like to take teddy or bunny along for the car ride?

Look for dialogue in blue for other examples of offering choices.

Give Encouragement

Let kids know you are proud of their efforts by offering specific words of encouragement. Instead of saying simply, "Good job!" notice and comment on what the child has done. "You put your crayons away before I even asked you to," or "You ate all your broccoli." Kids are much more likely to believe and react to specific encouragement.

Experts in child development point out that encouragement is different from praise. Praise—saying things like "Good job" or "Good girl"—conditions children to seek adults' approval rather than doing things for their own satisfaction. Praise focuses on the results of their efforts, assigns value to the results, and teaches kids they are only acceptable to you when they do well at things. Encouragement, on the other hand, focuses on their efforts and lets them know you love them and think they are important *no matter how well they perform*. For example, "You remembered to say please" encourages, whereas "Good job remembering your manners" praises.

Effective encouragement is also sincere. Here are some examples:

- You showed a lot of responsibility when you picked up your toys.
- Wow! You figured it out all by yourself.
- How did you do that? *or* Tell me how you did that!
- I can see why you are so proud.

Nonverbal gestures of encouragement also go a long way!

- a smile
- a pat on the shoulder or back
- a high five
- a hug

Look for dialogue in red for other examples of encouragement.

If the suggestions in this book feel unnatural or uncomfortable at first, try not to be intimidated! The father in this story uses many techniques in a short period of time in order to provide plenty of examples of the language of positive parenting. As a first step, try using the technique that seems most natural and comfortable for you. Repeated use over time will make the language more comfortable and lead to improved cooperation. Don't be discouraged if you don't see immediate changes in your family. It can take time, but it's worth it!

About the Author

Stacey R. Kaye, MMR, is the mother of two young children and a self-described "Parenting Lecture Groupie." As her first daughter grew into a feisty toddler, Stacey searched for a language she could use to discourage tantrums and meltdowns while at the same time encouraging her daughter to explore, gain confidence, and build emotional intelligence. Dozens of parenting tomes, lectures, and courses provided great theory, but not the language. That's when Stacey began writing ParentSmart/KidHappy books.

To learn more positive parenting tips and discover other ParentSmart/KidHappy titles, visit **www.ParentSmartKidHappy.com.**

Other Great Books from Free Spirit

Also in the ParentSmart/KidHappy™ Series

Ready for Bed!
A Tale of Cleaning Up, Tucking In, and Hardly Any Complaining
by Stacey R. Kaye, MMR
"I don't *want* to go to bed!" If you're a parent of a preschool-age child, you've probably heard this before. And you probably know about the crying, fits, and complaining—by both of you—that can follow. *Ready for Bed!* offers a healthy, lasting solution. Share this kid-friendly storybook with your child and you'll both learn a new, positive way to get through bedtime. Replace the begging, bribing, and brawling with positive parenting. Learn how working with kids in a respectful, give-and-take relationship gets better results and helps kids grow from the inside out. For ages 3–6.
$12.95; Hardcover; 32 pp.; color illust.; 8" x 8"

Words Are Not for Hurting
by Elizabeth Verdick
Even very young children can learn that their words affect other people in powerful ways. This book guides them to choose words that are helpful instead of hurtful, and to say "I'm sorry" when hurtful words come out before kids can stop them.
Paperback for ages 4–7. $11.95; 40 pp.; color illust.; 9" x 9".
Board book for ages baby–preschool. $7.95; 24 pp.; color illust.; 7" x 7".

Hands Are Not for Hitting
by Martine Agassi, Ph.D.
Little ones learn that violence is never okay, hands can do many good things, and everyone is capable of positive, loving actions.
Paperback for ages 4–7. $11.95; 40 pp.; color illust.; 9" x 9".
Board book for ages baby–preschool. $7.95; 24 pp.; color illust.; 7" x 7".

Free Spirit's Learning to Get Along® Series

by Cheri J. Meiners, M.Ed.

Help children learn, understand, and practice basic social and emotional skills. Real-life situations, diversity, and concrete examples make these read-aloud books appropriate for childcare settings, schools, and the home. *Each book: $10.95; S/C; 40 pp.; color illust.; 9" x 9"; ages 4–8.*

SERIES INCLUDES:

- Accept and Value Each Person
- Reach Out and Give
- Share and Take Turns
- Understand and Care
- Listen and Learn

- Be Careful and Stay Safe
- Try and Stick with It
- Know and Follow Rules
- When I Feel Afraid
- Join In and Play

- Talk and Work It Out
- Be Polite and Kind
- Respect and Take Care of Things
- Be Honest and Tell the Truth

To place an order or to request a free catalog of Self-Help for Kids® and Self-Help for Teens® materials, please write, call, email, or visit our Web site:

Free Spirit Publishing Inc.
217 Fifth Avenue North • Suite 200 • Minneapolis, MN 55401 • toll-free 800.735.7323 • local 612.338.2068
fax 612.337.5050 • help4kids@freespirit.com • www.freespirit.com

Fast, Friendly, and Easy to Use

www.freespirit.com

After breakfast, Maya helps clean up.
"We're a real team this morning," Daddy says.